OUR FAMILY TREE

A HISTORY
OF OUR FAMILY

POPLAR BOOKS

Our Family Tree

**Copyright © 1997, 2010 Poplar Books Inc.,
a division of Book Sales. Inc.
276 Fifth Ave, Suite 206
New York, NY 10001**

Library of Congress Card No. 77-78956
ISBN-13: 978-0-7858-2673-6
ISBN-10: 0-7858-2673-4
Manufactured in China

PICTURE CREDITS: BETTMANN ARCHIVE AND DOVER PUBLICATION: Handbook of Early Advertising Art.

10 9 8 7 6 5 4 3 2
Reprinted in 2011

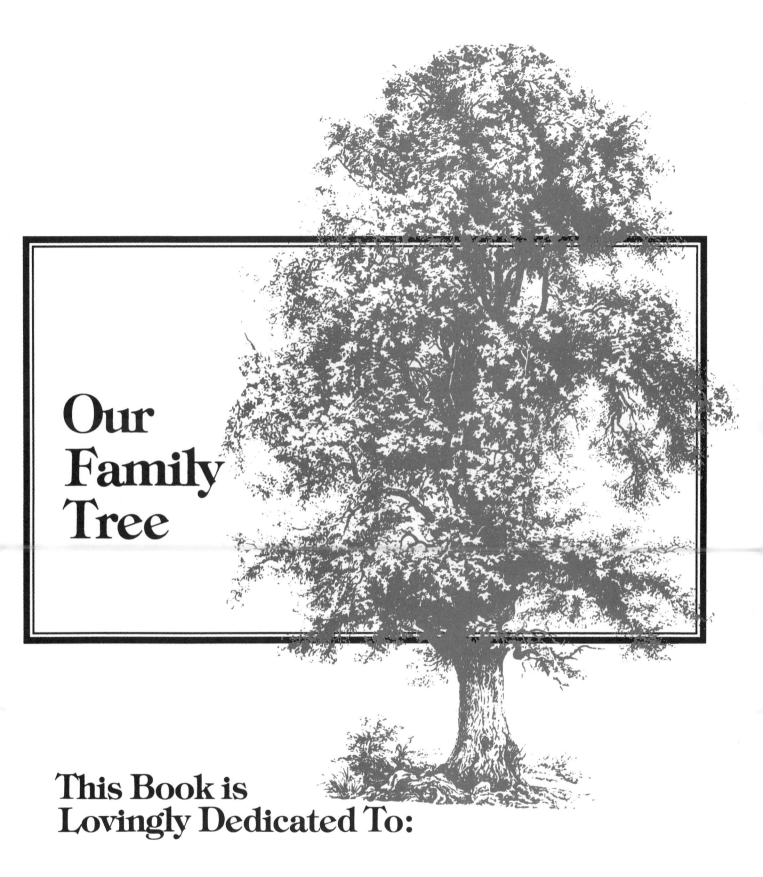

Our Family Tree

This Book is Lovingly Dedicated To:

_____

This Record was compiled by:

_____

_____

and started on _____

A family record is more than names, dates and places. It is about people—what they did, the why and the how. This book is designed so you can record forever, in one volume, the history of your family and your ancestors.

There are sections where you can enter the origins of your family: where your ancestors came from and when, what happened to them, and the things they did. You will also be able to record, perhaps for the first time, stories about members of your family that have been handed down from preceding generations. There are other sections devoted to family photographs, traditions and such memorable events as weddings and reunions. And there is a most important "how to" section that will help

you trace your family's history: where to write to obtain records, what information to include in such inquiries, and what institutions are available to you for further assistance (such as libraries and bookstores that specialize in genealogy information).

From the birth of a great, great grandparent to the birth of the newest baby in your family, this book provides a wonderful opportunity to gather together in one place all the interesting and unusual aspects of your family's history. When complete, it will be a storehouse of treasured information, achievements and memories—a permanent record of your family which is unique and not like any other.

CONTENTS

Our Family

This Certifies that

_____

And

_____

Were United in Holy Matrimony

Place of Ceremony _____

City _____ State _____

Month _____ Day _____ Year _____

Married by _____

_____

4

Husband's Genealogy

Husband's Full Name _____

_____

Birth Date _____

Birth Place _____

Father's Full Name _____

Mother's Full Name _____

Brothers and Sisters _____

_____

_____

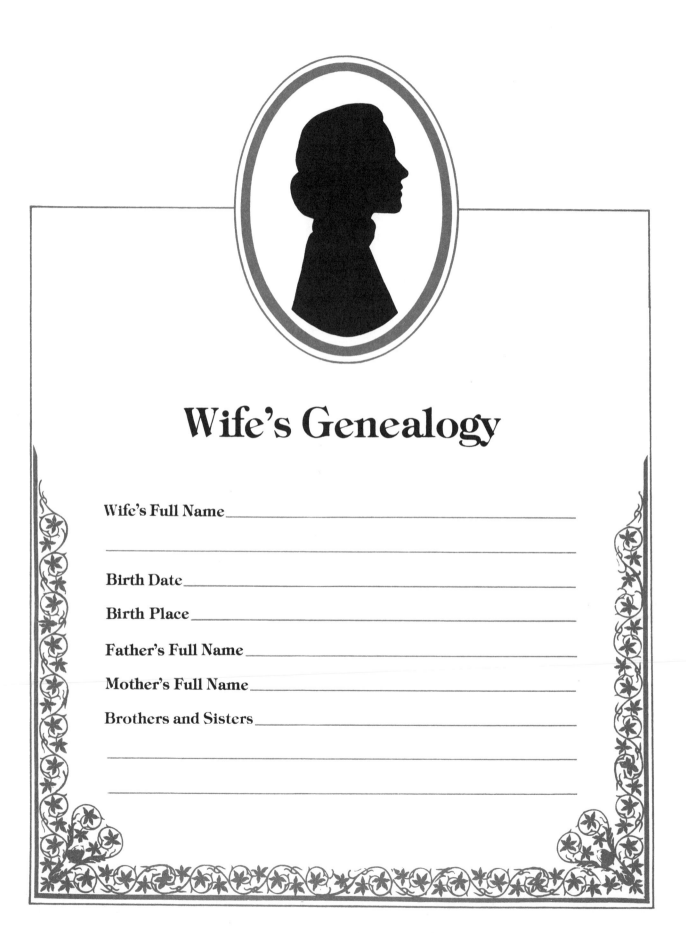

Wife's Genealogy

Wife's Full Name _____

_____

Birth Date _____

Birth Place _____

Father's Full Name _____

Mother's Full Name _____

Brothers and Sisters _____

_____

_____

Our Children

Full Name	Place of Birth	Date of Birth

Our Grandchildren and Descendants

_____
_____
_____
_____
_____
_____
_____
_____
_____
_____
_____
_____
_____
_____
_____
_____
_____
_____
_____
_____
_____
_____
_____
_____

Our Family Tree

HUSBAND'S FULL NAME

WIFE'S FULL NAME

DATE OF MARRIAGE   PLACE OF MARRIAGE

OUR CHILDREN

Who We Are and Who We Came From

HUSBAND'S PATERNAL GRANDFATHER'S FULL NAME

HUSBAND'S PATERNAL GRANDMOTHER'S FULL NAME

DATE OF MARRIAGE   PLACE OF MARRIAGE

CHILDREN

HUSBAND'S FATHER'S FULL NAME

HUSBAND'S MOTHER'S FULL NAME

DATE OF MARRIAGE   PLACE OF MARRIAGE

CHILDREN

HUSBAND'S MATERNAL GRANDFATHER'S FULL NAME

HUSBAND'S MATERNAL GRANDMOTHER'S FULL NAME

DATE OF MARRIAGE   PLACE OF MARRIAGE

CHILDREN

THE PRECEDING 3 GENERATIONS ON FOLLOWING PAGE ▶

WIFE'S PATERNAL GRANDFATHER'S FULL NAME

WIFE'S PATERNAL GRANDMOTHER'S FULL NAME

DATE OF MARRIAGE   PLACE OF MARRIAGE

CHILDREN

WIFE'S FATHER'S FULL NAME

WIFE'S MOTHER'S FULL NAME

DATE OF MARRIAGE   PLACE OF MARRIAGE

CHILDREN

WIFE'S MATERNAL GRANDFATHER'S FULL NAME

WIFE'S MATERNAL GRANDMOTHER'S FULL NAME

DATE OF MARRIAGE   PLACE OF MARRIAGE

CHILDREN

11

HUSBAND'S GREAT, GREAT GRANDFATHER'S FULL NAME

HUSBAND'S GREAT, GREAT GRANDMOTHER'S FULL NAME

HUSBAND'S GREAT GRANDFATHER'S FULL NAME

HUSBAND'S GREAT, GREAT GRANDFATHER'S FULL NAME

HUSBAND'S GREAT GRANDMOTHER'S FULL NAME

HUSBAND'S GREAT, GREAT GRANDMOTHER'S FULL NAME

HUSBAND'S GREAT, GREAT GRANDFATHER'S FULL NAME

HUSBAND'S GREAT, GREAT GRANDMOTHER'S FULL NAME

HUSBAND'S GREAT GRANDFATHER'S FULL NAME

HUSBAND'S GREAT, GREAT GRANDFATHER'S FULL NAME

HUSBAND'S GREAT GRANDMOTHER'S FULL NAME

HUSBAND'S GREAT, GREAT GRANDMOTHER'S FULL NAME

HUSBAND'S GREAT, GREAT GRANDFATHER'S FULL NAME

HUSBAND'S GREAT, GREAT GRANDMOTHER'S FULL NAME

HUSBAND'S GREAT GRANDFATHER'S FULL NAME

HUSBAND'S GREAT, GREAT GRANDFATHER'S FULL NAME

HUSBAND'S GREAT GRANDMOTHER'S FULL NAME

HUSBAND'S GREAT, GREAT GRANDMOTHER'S FULL NAME

HUSBAND'S GREAT, GREAT GRANDFATHER'S FULL NAME

HUSBAND'S GREAT, GREAT GRANDMOTHER'S FULL NAME

HUSBAND'S GREAT GRANDFATHER'S FULL NAME

HUSBAND'S GREAT, GREAT GRANDFATHER'S FULL NAME

HUSBAND'S GREAT GRANDMOTHER'S FULL NAME

HUSBAND'S GREAT, GREAT GRANDMOTHER'S FULL NAME

WIFE'S GREAT, GREAT GRANDFATHER'S FULL NAME

WIFE'S GREAT, GREAT GRANDMOTHER'S FULL NAME

WIFE'S GREAT GRANDFATHER'S FULL NAME

WIFE'S GREAT, GREAT GRANDFATHER'S FULL NAME

WIFE'S GREAT GRANDMOTHER'S FULL NAME

WIFE'S GREAT, GREAT GRANDMOTHER'S FULL NAME

WIFE'S GREAT, GREAT GRANDFATHER'S FULL NAME

WIFE'S GREAT, GREAT GRANDMOTHER'S FULL NAME

WIFE'S GREAT GRANDFATHER'S FULL NAME

WIFE'S GREAT, GREAT GRANDFATHER'S FULL NAME

WIFE'S GREAT GRANDMOTHER'S FULL NAME

WIFE'S GREAT, GREAT GRANDMOTHER'S FULL NAME

WIFE'S GREAT, GREAT GRANDFATHER'S FULL NAME

WIFE'S GREAT, GREAT GRANDMOTHER'S FULL NAME

WIFE'S GREAT GRANDFATHER'S FULL NAME

WIFE'S GREAT, GREAT GRANDFATHER'S FULL NAME

WIFE'S GREAT GRANDMOTHER'S FULL NAME

WIFE'S GREAT, GREAT GRANDMOTHER'S FULL NAME

WIFE'S GREAT, GREAT GRANDFATHER'S FULL NAME

WIFE'S GREAT, GREAT GRANDMOTHER'S FULL NAME

WIFE'S GREAT GRANDFATHER'S FULL NAME

WIFE'S GREAT, GREAT GRANDFATHER'S FULL NAME

WIFE'S GREAT GRANDMOTHER'S FULL NAME

WIFE'S GREAT, GREAT GRANDMOTHER'S FULL NAME

Great, Great, Great Grandparents

MR. & MRS. _____ NEE _____

MR. & MRS. _____ NEE _____

MR. & MRS. _____ NEE _____

MR. & MRS. _____ NEE _____

MR. & MRS. _____ NEE _____

MR. & MRS. _____ NEE _____

MR. & MRS. _____ NEE _____

MR. & MRS. _____ NEE _____

MR. & MRS. _____ NEE _____

MR. & MRS. _____ NEE _____

MR. & MRS. _____ NEE _____

MR. & MRS. _____ NEE _____

MR. & MRS. _____ NEE _____

MR. & MRS. _____ NEE _____

MR. & MRS. _____ NEE _____

MR. & MRS. _____ NEE _____

MR. & MRS. _____ NEE _____

MR. & MRS. _____ NEE _____

MR. & MRS. _____ NEE _____

MR. & MRS. _____ NEE _____

MR. & MRS. _____ NEE _____

MR. & MRS. _____ NEE _____

MR. & MRS. _____ NEE _____

MR. & MRS. _____ NEE _____

MR. & MRS. _____ NEE _____

MR. & MRS. _____ NEE _____

MR. & MRS. _____ NEE _____

MR. & MRS. _____ NEE _____

MR. & MRS. _____ NEE _____

MR. & MRS. _____ NEE _____

MR. & MRS. _____ NEE _____

MR. & MRS. _____ NEE _____

NEE REPRESENTS WIFE'S MAIDEN NAME

The generations preceding the one in the column on the left would have been born about 1800 and of course would be double the number.

Each generation going back in time will be twice the number. If your ancestors landed here in 1600 and you are under 30, you would be the 14th or 15th generation and be descended from over 16,000 people.

For a variety of reasons, families have altered the spelling of the last name or changed it completely. So in looking back and trying to get information from the county, city or town overseas that your family came from, make sure you include as much data as you can get before writing abroad.

13

Husband's Ancestral Chart

HUSBAND'S FULL NAME

DATE OF BIRTH   PLACE OF BIRTH

DATE OF MARRIAGE   PLACE OF MARRIAGE

DATE OF DEATH   PLACE OF BURIAL

OCCUPATION

SPECIAL INTERESTS

GRANDFATHER'S FULL NAME

DATE OF BIRTH   PLACE OF BIRTH

DATE OF MARRIAGE   PLACE OF MARRIAGE

DATE OF DEATH   PLACE OF BURIAL

OCCUPATION

SPECIAL INTERESTS

FATHER'S FULL NAME

DATE OF BIRTH   PLACE OF BIRTH

DATE OF MARRIAGE   PLACE OF MARRIAGE

DATE OF DEATH   PLACE OF BURIAL

OCCUPATION

SPECIAL INTERESTS

GRANDMOTHER'S FULL NAME

DATE OF BIRTH   PLACE OF BIRTH

DATE OF MARRIAGE   PLACE OF MARRIAGE

DATE OF DEATH   PLACE OF BURIAL

OCCUPATION

SPECIAL INTERESTS

THE PRECEDING 3 GENERATIONS ON FOLLOWING PAGE

GRANDFATHER'S FULL NAME

DATE OF BIRTH   PLACE OF BIRTH

DATE OF MARRIAGE   PLACE OF MARRIAGE

DATE OF DEATH   PLACE OF BURIAL

OCCUPATION

SPECIAL INTERESTS

MOTHER'S FULL NAME

DATE OF BIRTH   PLACE OF BIRTH

DATE OF MARRIAGE   PLACE OF MARRIAGE

DATE OF DEATH   PLACE OF BURIAL

OCCUPATION

SPECIAL INTERESTS

GRANDMOTHER'S FULL NAME

DATE OF BIRTH   PLACE OF BIRTH

DATE OF MARRIAGE   PLACE OF MARRIAGE

DATE OF DEATH   PLACE OF BURIAL

OCCUPATION

SPECIAL INTERESTS

GREAT GRANDFATHER'S FULL NAME

DATE OF BIRTH   PLACE OF BIRTH

OCCUPATION

GREAT GRANDMOTHER'S FULL NAME

DATE OF BIRTH   PLACE OF BIRTH

SPECIAL INTERESTS

GREAT GRANDFATHER'S FULL NAME

DATE OF BIRTH   PLACE OF BIRTH

OCCUPATION

GREAT GRANDMOTHER'S FULL NAME

DATE OF BIRTH   PLACE OF BIRTH

SPECIAL INTERESTS

GREAT GRANDFATHER'S FULL NAME

DATE OF BIRTH   PLACE OF BIRTH

OCCUPATION

GREAT GRANDMOTHER'S FULL NAME

DATE OF BIRTH   PLACE OF BIRTH

SPECIAL INTERESTS

GREAT GRANDFATHER'S FULL NAME

DATE OF BIRTH   PLACE OF BIRTH

OCCUPATION

GREAT GRANDMOTHER'S FULL NAME

DATE OF BIRTH   PLACE OF BIRTH

SPECIAL INTERESTS

GREAT, GREAT GRANDFATHER'S FULL NAME

GREAT, GREAT GRANDMOTHER'S FULL NAME

GREAT, GREAT GRANDFATHER'S FULL NAME

GREAT, GREAT GRANDMOTHER'S FULL NAME

GREAT, GREAT GRANDFATHER'S FULL NAME

GREAT, GREAT GRANDMOTHER'S FULL NAME

GREAT, GREAT GRANDFATHER'S FULL NAME

GREAT, GREAT GRANDMOTHER'S FULL NAME

GREAT, GREAT GRANDFATHER'S FULL NAME

GREAT, GREAT GRANDMOTHER'S FULL NAME

GREAT, GREAT GRANDFATHER'S FULL NAME

GREAT, GREAT GRANDMOTHER'S FULL NAME

GREAT, GREAT GRANDFATHER'S FULL NAME

GREAT, GREAT GRANDMOTHER'S FULL NAME

GREAT, GREAT GRANDFATHER'S FULL NAME

GREAT, GREAT GRANDMOTHER'S FULL NAME

Great, Great, Great Grandparents

MR. & MRS. _____ NEE _____
MR. & MRS. _____ NEE _____

MR. & MRS. _____ NEE _____
MR. & MRS. _____ NEE _____

MR. & MRS. _____ NEE _____
MR. & MRS. _____ NEE _____

MR. & MRS. _____ NEE _____
MR. & MRS. _____ NEE _____

MR. & MRS. _____ NEE _____
MR. & MRS. _____ NEE _____

MR. & MRS. _____ NEE _____
MR. & MRS. _____ NEE _____

MR. & MRS. _____ NEE _____
MR. & MRS. _____ NEE _____

MR. & MRS. _____ NEE _____
MR. & MRS. _____ NEE _____

MR. & MRS. _____ NEE _____
MR. & MRS. _____ NEE _____

MR. & MRS. _____ NEE _____
MR. & MRS. _____ NEE _____

MR. & MRS. _____ NEE _____
MR. & MRS. _____ NEE _____

MR. & MRS. _____ NEE _____
MR. & MRS. _____ NEE _____

MR. & MRS. _____ NEE _____
MR. & MRS. _____ NEE _____

MR. & MRS. _____ NEE _____
MR. & MRS. _____ NEE _____

MR. & MRS. _____ NEE _____
MR. & MRS. _____ NEE _____

NEE REPRESENTS WIFE'S MAIDEN NAME

17

Husband's Family

On this and the next page, fill in all vital statistics on the husband, his brothers and sisters, and their children (nieces and nephews).

**Husband,
his Brothers and Sisters,
and their Children**

	BORN	DIED	SPOUSE
Children			
Children			
Children			
Children			
Children			
Children			
Children			
Children			
Children			

Legal Guardians

(FILL IN NAMES OF LEGAL GUARDIANS FOR ANY CHILD WHERE APPLICABLE. INCLUDING DATES, PLACES AND ANY INFORMATION YOU CONSIDER APPROPRIATE.)

Husband's Parents' Family

On this and the following pages, fill in all vital statistics on the husband's parents, their brothers and sisters (aunts and uncles), and their children (cousins).

**Husband's Father,
his Brothers and Sisters,
and their Children**

	BORN	DIED	SPOUSE
Children			
Children			
Children			
Children			
Children			
Children			
Children			
Children			
Children			
Children			

Legal Guardians

(FILL IN NAMES OF LEGAL GUARDIANS FOR ANY CHILD WHERE APPLICABLE. INCLUDING DATES. PLACES AND ANY INFORMATION YOU CONSIDER APPROPRIATE.)

21

Husband's Parents' Family

CONTINUED

**Husband's Mother,
her Brothers and Sisters,
and their Children**

	BORN	DIED	SPOUSE
Children			
Children			
Children			
Children			
Children			
Children			
Children			
Children			
Children			

Legal Guardians

(FILL IN NAMES OF LEGAL GUARDIANS FOR ANY CHILD WHERE APPLICABLE. INCLUDING DATES, PLACES AND ANY INFORMATION YOU CONSIDER APPROPRIATE.)

Husband's Grandparents—Father's Side

**Grandfather,
his Brothers and Sisters,
and their Children**

	BORN	DIED	SPOUSE
Children			
Children			
Children			
Children			
Children			
Children			
Children			
Children			
Children			

Legal Guardians

(FILL IN NAMES OF LEGAL GUARDIANS FOR ANY CHILD WHERE APPLICABLE INCLUDING DATES PLACES AND ANY INFORMATION YOU CONSIDER APPROPRIATE.)

Husband's Grandparents— Father's Side

CONTINUED

Grandmother, her Brothers and Sisters, and their Children

	BORN	DIED	SPOUSE
Children			
Children			
Children			
Children			
Children			
Children			
Children			
Children			
Children			

Legal Guardians

(FILL IN NAMES OF LEGAL GUARDIANS FOR ANY CHILD WHERE APPLICABLE. INCLUDING DATES, PLACES AND ANY INFORMATION YOU CONSIDER APPROPRIATE.)

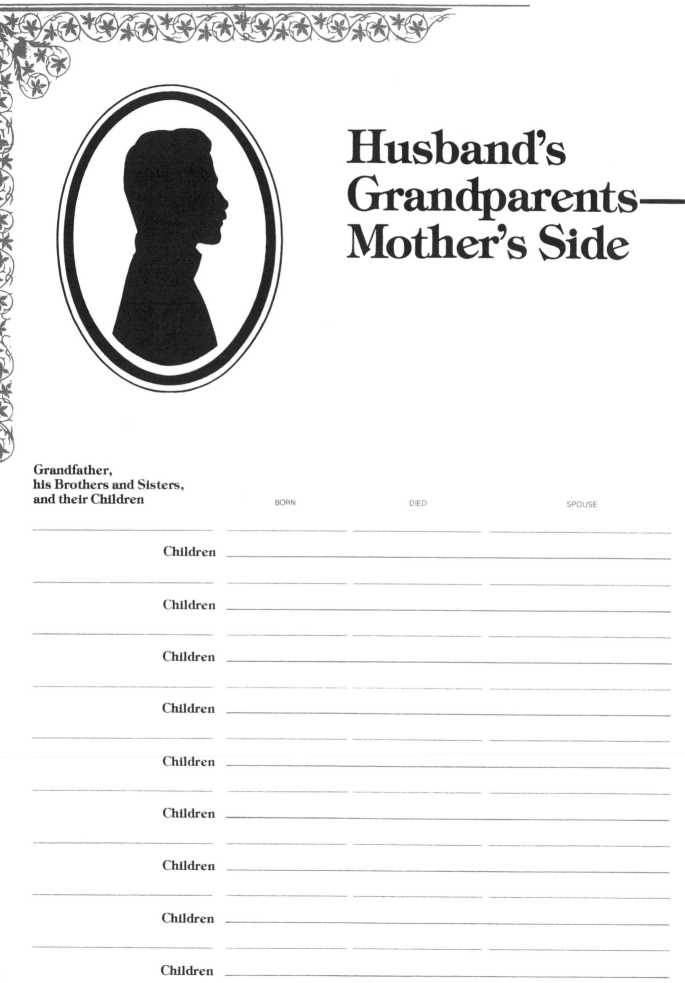

Husband's Grandparents— Mother's Side

**Grandfather,
his Brothers and Sisters,
and their Children**

	BORN	DIED	SPOUSE
Children			
Children			
Children			
Children			
Children			
Children			
Children			
Children			
Children			

Legal Guardians

(FILL IN NAMES OF LEGAL GUARDIANS FOR ANY CHILD WHERE APPLICABLE INCLUDING DATES, PLACES AND ANY INFORMATION YOU CONSIDER APPROPRIATE.)

Husband's Grandparents— Mother's Side

CONTINUED

**Grandmother,
her Brothers and Sisters,
and their Children**

	BORN	DIED	SPOUSE
Children			
Children			
Children			
Children			
Children			
Children			
Children			
Children			
Children			

Legal Guardians

(FILL IN NAMES OF LEGAL GUARDIANS FOR ANY CHILD WHERE APPLICABLE. INCLUDING DATES, PLACES AND ANY INFORMATION YOU CONSIDER APPROPRIATE.)

Husband's Great Grandparents

NAME	BORN	DIED	SPOUSE
Children			
Children			
Children			
Children			
Children			
Children			
Children			
Children			
Children			

Legal Guardians

33

Wife's Ancestral Chart

WIFE'S FULL NAME

DATE OF BIRTH   PLACE OF BIRTH

DATE OF MARRIAGE   PLACE OF MARRIAGE

DATE OF DEATH   PLACE OF BURIAL

OCCUPATION

SPECIAL INTERESTS

GRANDFATHER'S FULL NAME

DATE OF BIRTH   PLACE OF BIRTH

DATE OF MARRIAGE   PLACE OF MARRIAGE

DATE OF DEATH   PLACE OF BURIAL

OCCUPATION

SPECIAL INTERESTS

FATHER'S FULL NAME

DATE OF BIRTH   PLACE OF BIRTH

DATE OF MARRIAGE   PLACE OF MARRIAGE

DATE OF DEATH   PLACE OF BURIAL

OCCUPATION

SPECIAL INTERESTS

GRANDMOTHER'S FULL NAME

DATE OF BIRTH   PLACE OF BIRTH

DATE OF MARRIAGE   PLACE OF MARRIAGE

DATE OF DEATH   PLACE OF BURIAL

OCCUPATION

SPECIAL INTERESTS

THE PRECEDING 3 GENERATIONS ON FOLLOWING PAGE

GRANDFATHER'S FULL NAME

DATE OF BIRTH   PLACE OF BIRTH

DATE OF MARRIAGE   PLACE OF MARRIAGE

DATE OF DEATH   PLACE OF BURIAL

OCCUPATION

SPECIAL INTERESTS

MOTHER'S FULL NAME

DATE OF BIRTH   PLACE OF BIRTH

DATE OF MARRIAGE   PLACE OF MARRIAGE

DATE OF DEATH   PLACE OF BURIAL

OCCUPATION

SPECIAL INTERESTS

GRANDMOTHER'S FULL NAME

DATE OF BIRTH   PLACE OF BIRTH

DATE OF MARRIAGE   PLACE OF MARRIAGE

DATE OF DEATH   PLACE OF BURIAL

OCCUPATION

SPECIAL INTERESTS

GREAT GRANDFATHER'S FULL NAME

DATE OF BIRTH   PLACE OF BIRTH

OCCUPATION

GREAT GRANDMOTHER'S FULL NAME

DATE OF BIRTH   PLACE OF BIRTH

SPECIAL INTERESTS

GREAT GRANDFATHER'S FULL NAME

DATE OF BIRTH   PLACE OF BIRTH

OCCUPATION

GREAT GRANDMOTHER'S FULL NAME

DATE OF BIRTH   PLACE OF BIRTH

SPECIAL INTERESTS

GREAT GRANDFATHER'S FULL NAME

DATE OF BIRTH   PLACE OF BIRTH

OCCUPATION

GREAT GRANDMOTHER'S FULL NAME

DATE OF BIRTH   PLACE OF BIRTH

SPECIAL INTERESTS

GREAT GRANDFATHER'S FULL NAME

DATE OF BIRTH   PLACE OF BIRTH

OCCUPATION

GREAT GRANDMOTHER'S FULL NAME

DATE OF BIRTH   PLACE OF BIRTH

SPECIAL INTERESTS

GREAT, GREAT GRANDFATHER'S FULL NAME

GREAT, GREAT GRANDMOTHER'S FULL NAME

GREAT, GREAT GRANDFATHER'S FULL NAME

GREAT, GREAT GRANDMOTHER'S FULL NAME

GREAT, GREAT GRANDFATHER'S FULL NAME

GREAT, GREAT GRANDMOTHER'S FULL NAME

GREAT, GREAT GRANDFATHER'S FULL NAME

GREAT, GREAT GRANDMOTHER'S FULL NAME

GREAT, GREAT GRANDFATHER'S FULL NAME

GREAT, GREAT GRANDMOTHER'S FULL NAME

GREAT, GREAT GRANDFATHER'S FULL NAME

GREAT, GREAT GRANDMOTHER'S FULL NAME

GREAT, GREAT GRANDFATHER'S FULL NAME

GREAT, GREAT GRANDMOTHER'S FULL NAME

GREAT, GREAT GRANDFATHER'S FULL NAME

GREAT, GREAT GRANDMOTHER'S FULL NAME

Great, Great, Great Grandparents

MR. & MRS. _____ NEE _____
MR. & MRS. _____ NEE _____

MR. & MRS. _____ NEE _____
MR. & MRS. _____ NEE _____

MR. & MRS. _____ NEE _____
MR. & MRS. _____ NEE _____

MR. & MRS. _____ NEE _____
MR. & MRS. _____ NEE _____

MR. & MRS. _____ NEE _____
MR. & MRS. _____ NEE _____

MR. & MRS. _____ NEE _____
MR. & MRS. _____ NEE _____

MR. & MRS. _____ NEE _____
MR. & MRS. _____ NEE _____

MR. & MRS. _____ NEE _____
MR. & MRS. _____ NEE _____

MR. & MRS. _____ NEE _____
MR. & MRS. _____ NEE _____

MR. & MRS. _____ NEE _____
MR. & MRS. _____ NEE _____

MR. & MRS. _____ NEE _____
MR. & MRS. _____ NEE _____

MR. & MRS. _____ NEE _____
MR. & MRS. _____ NEE _____

MR. & MRS. _____ NEE _____
MR. & MRS. _____ NEE _____

MR. & MRS. _____ NEE _____
MR. & MRS. _____ NEE _____

MR. & MRS. _____ NEE _____
MR. & MRS. _____ NEE _____

NEE REPRESENTS WIFE'S MAIDEN NAME

Wife's Family

On this and the next page, fill in all vital statistics on the wife, her brothers and sisters, and their children (nieces and nephews).

**Wife,
her Brothers and Sisters,
and their Children**

	BORN	DIED	SPOUSE
Children			
Children			
Children			
Children			
Children			
Children			
Children			
Children			
Children			
Children			

Legal Guardians

(FILL IN NAMES OF LEGAL GUARDIANS FOR ANY CHILD WHERE APPLICABLE. INCLUDING DATES. PLACES AND ANY INFORMATION YOU CONSIDER APPROPRIATE.)

Wife's Parents' Family

On this and the following pages, fill in all vital statistics on the wife's parents, their brothers and sisters (aunts and uncles), and their children (cousins).

**Wife's Father,
his Brothers and Sisters,
and their Children**

	BORN	DIED	SPOUSE
Children			
Children			
Children			
Children			
Children			
Children			
Children			
Children			
Children			

Legal Guardians

(FILL IN NAMES OF LEGAL GUARDIANS FOR ANY CHILD WHERE APPLICABLE. INCLUDING DATES. PLACES AND ANY INFORMATION YOU CONSIDER APPROPRIATE.)

41

Wife's Parents' Family <small>CONTINUED</small>

**Wife's Mother,
her Brothers and Sisters,
and their Children**

	BORN	DIED	SPOUSE
Children			
Children			
Children			
Children			
Children			
Children			
Children			
Children			
Children			

Legal Guardians

(FILL IN NAMES OF LEGAL GUARDIANS FOR ANY CHILD WHERE APPLICABLE, INCLUDING DATES, PLACES AND ANY INFORMATION YOU CONSIDER APPROPRIATE.)

43

Wife's Grandparents— Father's Side

**Grandfather,
his Brothers and Sisters,
and their Children**

	BORN	DIED	SPOUSE
_____	_____	_____	_____
Children	_____	_____	_____
_____	_____	_____	_____
Children	_____	_____	_____
_____	_____	_____	_____
Children	_____	_____	_____
_____	_____	_____	_____
Children	_____	_____	_____
_____	_____	_____	_____
Children	_____	_____	_____
_____	_____	_____	_____
Children	_____	_____	_____
_____	_____	_____	_____
Children	_____	_____	_____
_____	_____	_____	_____
Children	_____	_____	_____
_____	_____	_____	_____
Children	_____	_____	_____

Legal Guardians

(FILL IN NAMES OF LEGAL GUARDIANS FOR ANY CHILD WHERE APPLICABLE, INCLUDING DATES, PLACES AND ANY INFORMATION YOU CONSIDER APPROPRIATE.)

Wife's Grandparents— Father's Side

CONTINUED

Grandmother, her Brothers and Sisters, and their Children

	BORN	DIED	SPOUSE
Children			
Children			
Children			
Children			
Children			
Children			
Children			
Children			
Children			

Legal Guardians

(FILL IN NAMES OF LEGAL GUARDIANS FOR ANY CHILD WHERE APPLICABLE. INCLUDING DATES. PLACES AND ANY INFORMATION YOU CONSIDER APPROPRIATE.)

Wife's Grandparents— Mother's Side

**Grandfather,
his Brothers and Sisters,
and their Children**

	BORN	DIED	SPOUSE
Children			
Children			
Children			
Children			
Children			
Children			
Children			
Children			
Children			

48

Legal Guardians

(FILL IN NAMES OF LEGAL GUARDIANS FOR ANY CHILD WHERE APPLICABLE. INCLUDING DATES. PLACES AND ANY INFORMATION YOU CONSIDER APPROPRIATE.)

Wife's Grandparents— Mother's Side

CONTINUED

**Grandmother,
her Brothers and Sisters,
and their Children**

	BORN	DIED	SPOUSE
Children			
Children			
Children			
Children			
Children			
Children			
Children			
Children			
Children			

Legal Guardians

(FILL IN NAMES OF LEGAL GUARDIANS FOR ANY CHILD WHERE APPLICABLE. INCLUDING DATES, PLACES AND ANY INFORMATION YOU CONSIDER APPROPRIATE.)

Wife's Great Grandparents

NAME	BORN	DIED	SPOUSE
Children			
Children			
Children			
Children			
Children			
Children			
Children			
Children			
Children			
Children			

Legal Guardians
(FILL IN NAMES OF LEGAL GUARDIANS FOR ANY CHILD WHERE APPLICABLE. INCLUDING DATES. PLACES AND ANY INFORMATION YOU CONSIDER APPROPRIATE.)

NAME	EMIGRATED FROM	TO	DATE

Citizenship Record

In the space below fill in the countries your family came from along with any other information about that place you have or can get. Also put in when the family emigrated, where they landed and how your branch settled where it is now.

NAME	EMIGRATED FROM	TO	DATE

Citizenship Record CONTINUED

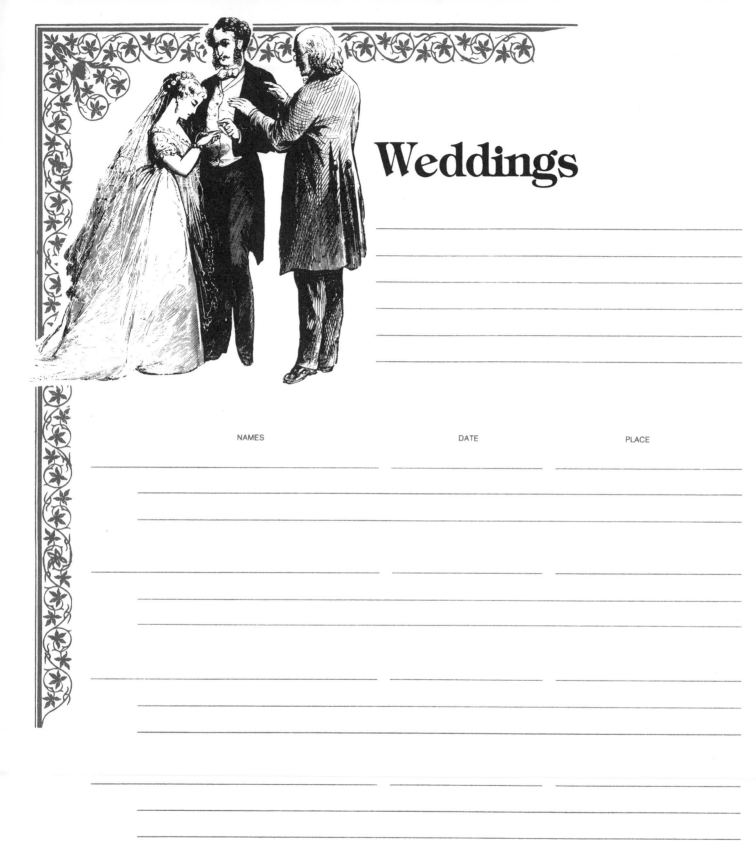

Weddings

_____
_____
_____
_____
_____
_____

NAMES	DATE	PLACE

NAMES	DATE	PLACE

Weddings CONTINUED

_____

_____

_____

_____

_____

_____

_____

_____

_____

_____

_____

_____

_____

_____

_____

_____

_____

_____

_____

_____

_____

_____

_____

_____

_____

_____

_____

_____

Religious Activities

_____

_____

_____

_____

_____

NAME	CEREMONY OR OCCASION	GODPARENTS OR SPONSORS	DATE & PLACE

NAME	CEREMONY OR OCCASION	GODPARENTS OR SPONSORS	DATE & PLACE

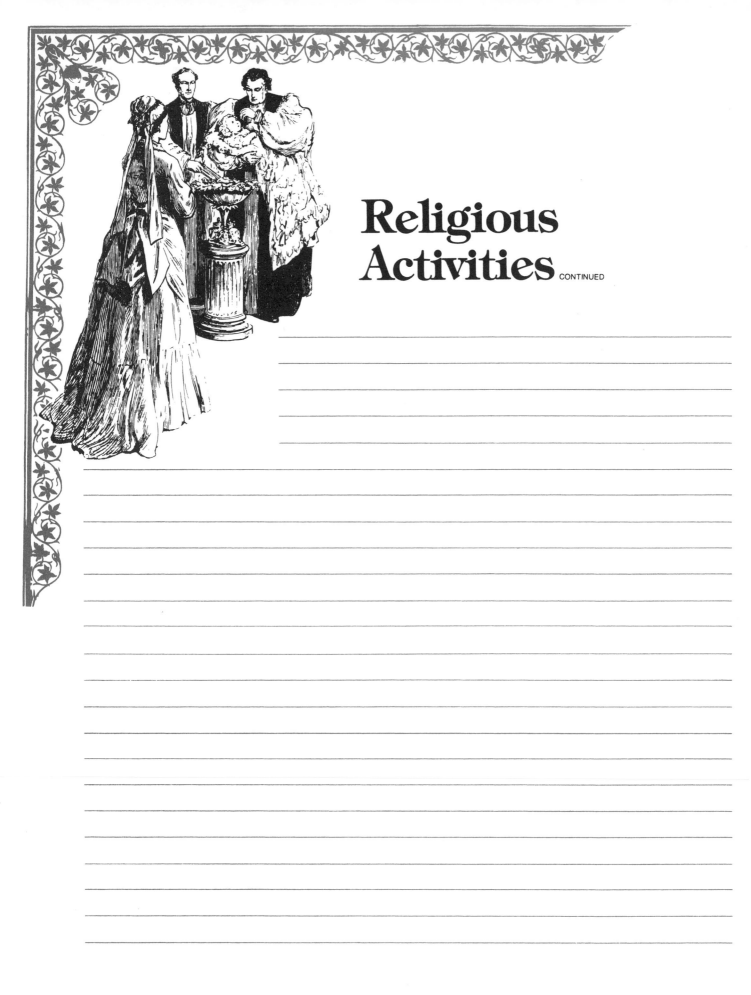

Religious Activities CONTINUED

Our Places
of Worship

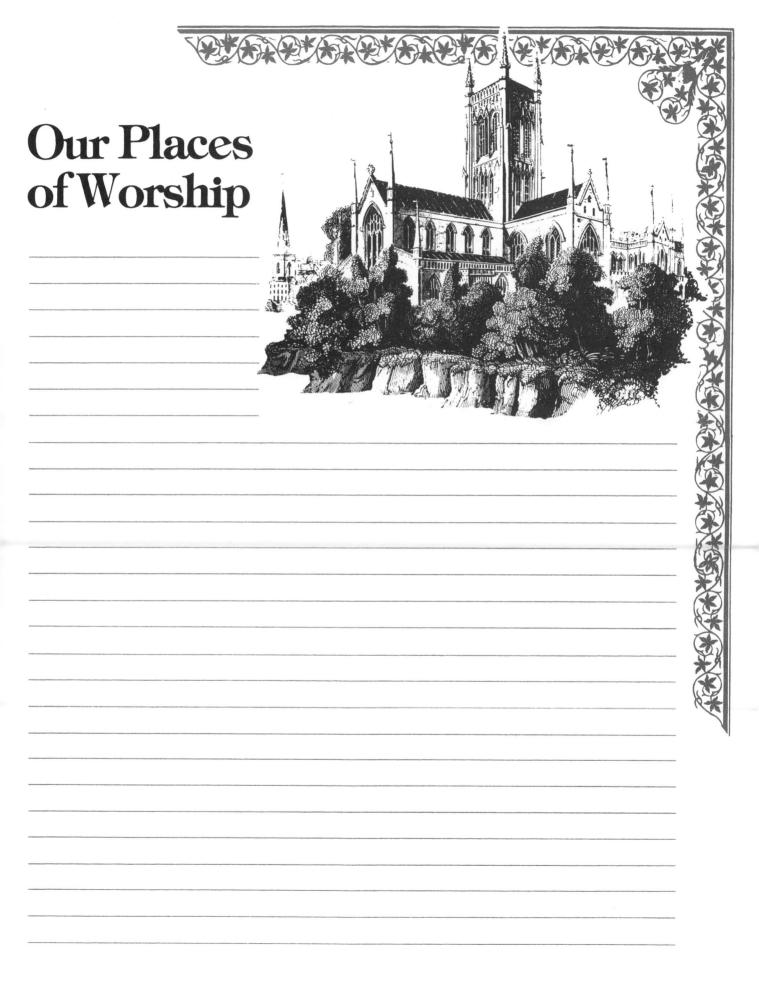

_____
_____
_____
_____
_____
_____
_____
_____
_____
_____
_____
_____
_____
_____
_____
_____
_____
_____
_____
_____
_____
_____
_____
_____
_____
_____
_____
_____
_____

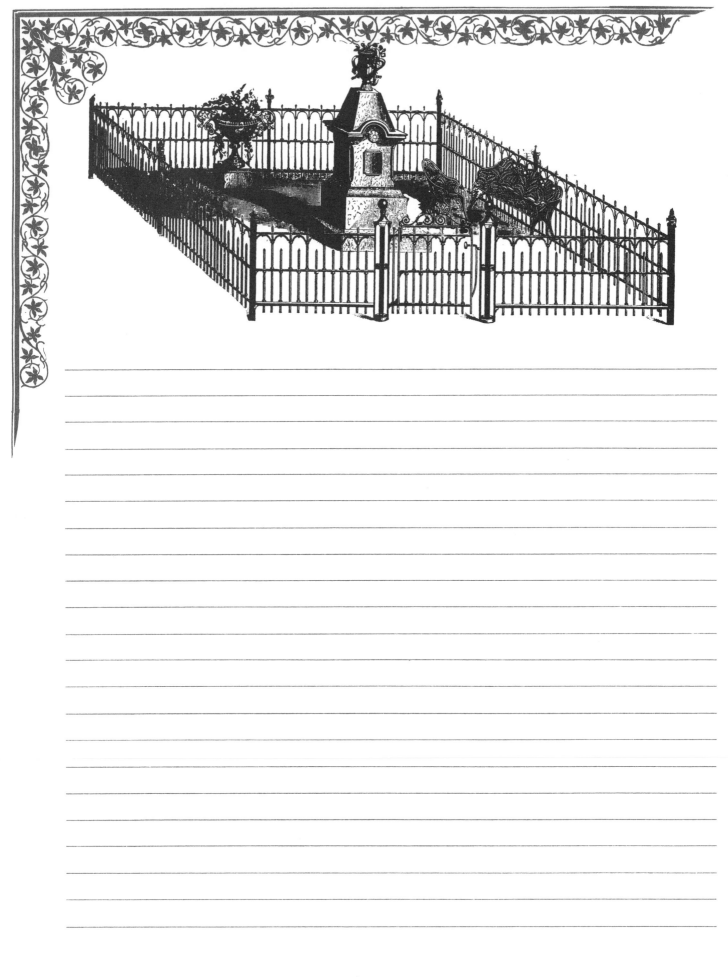

In Memoriam

Here you may record names of those who have
died about whom you have special memories. You
may write stories you have heard or your own
personal thoughts.

In Memoriam

CONTINUED

Our Homes

Street Address _____

City _____ State _____

Date of Purchase _____ Resided from _____ to _____

_____

_____

_____

_____

_____

_____

_____

Street Address _____

City _____ State _____

Date of Purchase _____ Resided from _____ to _____

_____

_____

_____

_____

_____

_____

_____

Street Address ———————————————————————————————————————

City ————————————————————————————— State ——————————————

Date of Purchase —————————————— Resided from ——————————— to ——————————

——

——

——

——

——

——

Street Address ———————————————————————————————————————

City ————————————————————————————— State ——————————————

Date of Purchase —————————————— Resided from ——————————— to ——————————

——

——

——

——

——

——

Street Address ———————————————————————————————————————

City ————————————————————————————— State ——————————————

Date of Purchase —————————————— Resided from ——————————— to ——————————

——

——

——

——

——

——

Street Address _____

City _____ State _____

Date of Purchase _____ Resided from _____ to _____

_____

_____

_____

_____

_____

_____

_____

Street Address _____

City _____ State _____

Date of Purchase _____ Resided from _____ to _____

_____

_____

_____

_____

_____

_____

_____

Street Address _____

City _____ State _____

Date of Purchase _____ Resided from _____ to _____

_____

_____

_____

_____

_____

Where Our Ancestors Have Lived

Schools

NAME	SCHOOL, COLLEGE OR UNIVERSITY	DATES OF ATTENDANCE	CERTIFICATE OR DEGREE

and Graduations

Schools and Graduations CONTINUED

Important School Achievements—Fine Arts, Athletics and Others

NAME	ACHIEVEMENT	DATE	SCHOOL

Clubs and Organizations

NAME	ORGANIZATION	ACTIVITY, AWARD, OFFICE HELD	DATE

Fill in names of family members and their clubs and organizations, including offices held and any other interesting information about the person or the organization.

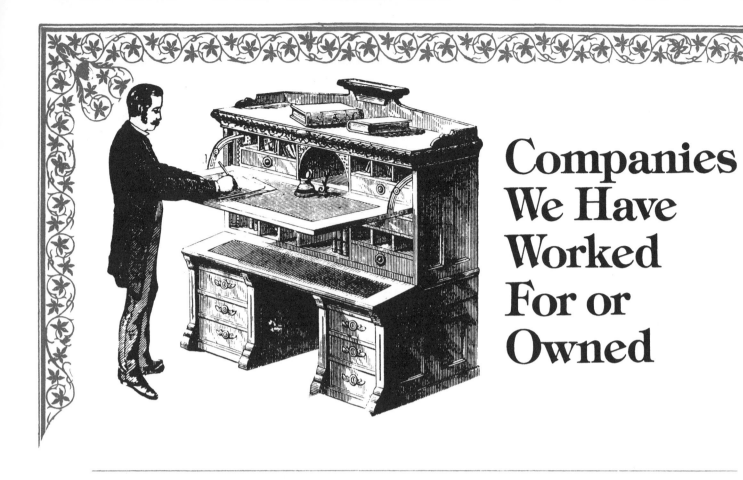

Companies
We Have
Worked
For or
Owned

You may record here employment histories and
businesses started by any member of your family,
including when and where a business was begun,
and its success or failure and why.

_____
_____
_____
_____
_____
_____
_____
_____
_____
_____
_____
_____
_____
_____
_____
_____
_____
_____
_____
_____
_____
_____
_____
_____
_____

Companies We Have Worked For or Owned

CONTINUED

Social Security Numbers

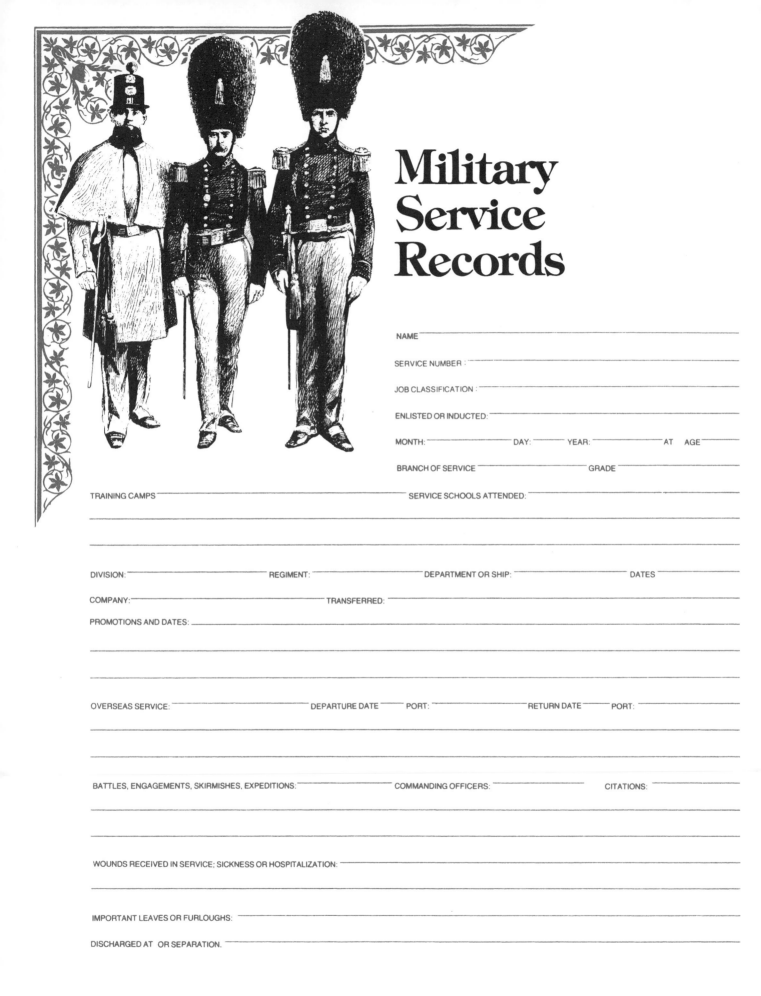

Military Service Records

NAME

SERVICE NUMBER :

JOB CLASSIFICATION :

ENLISTED OR INDUCTED:

MONTH: DAY: YEAR: AT AGE

BRANCH OF SERVICE GRADE

TRAINING CAMPS SERVICE SCHOOLS ATTENDED:

DIVISION: REGIMENT: DEPARTMENT OR SHIP: DATES

COMPANY: TRANSFERRED:

PROMOTIONS AND DATES:

OVERSEAS SERVICE: DEPARTURE DATE PORT: RETURN DATE PORT:

BATTLES, ENGAGEMENTS, SKIRMISHES, EXPEDITIONS: COMMANDING OFFICERS: CITATIONS:

WOUNDS RECEIVED IN SERVICE; SICKNESS OR HOSPITALIZATION:

IMPORTANT LEAVES OR FURLOUGHS:

DISCHARGED AT OR SEPARATION.

NAME _____ SERVICE NUMBER: _____ JOB CLASSIFICATION: _____

ENLISTED OR INDUCTED: _____ MONTH: _____ DAY: _____ YEAR: _____ AT AGE _____

BRANCH OF SERVICE _____ GRADE _____

TRAINING CAMPS _____ SERVICE SCHOOLS ATTENDED: _____

_____

_____

_____

DIVISION: _____ REGIMENT: _____ DEPARTMENT OR SHIP: _____ DATES _____

COMPANY: _____ TRANSFERRED: _____

_____

PROMOTIONS AND DATES: _____

_____

_____

_____

_____

OVERSEAS SERVICE: _____ DEPARTURE DATE _____ PORT: _____ RETURN DATE _____ PORT: _____

_____

_____

_____

_____

BATTLES, ENGAGEMENTS, SKIRMISHES, EXPEDITIONS: _____ COMMANDING OFFICERS: _____ CITATIONS: _____

_____

_____

_____

_____

WOUNDS RECEIVED IN SERVICE; SICKNESS OR HOSPITALIZATION: _____

_____

_____

IMPORTANT LEAVES OR FURLOUGHS: _____

_____

DISCHARGED AT OR SEPARATION. _____

Military Service Records CONTINUED

NAME

SERVICE NUMBER:

JOB CLASSIFICATION:

ENLISTED OR INDUCTED:

MONTH: DAY: YEAR: AT   AGE

BRANCH OF SERVICE   GRADE

TRAINING CAMPS   SERVICE SCHOOLS ATTENDED:

DIVISION: REGIMENT: DEPARTMENT OR SHIP: DATES

COMPANY: TRANSFERRED:

PROMOTIONS AND DATES:

OVERSEAS SERVICE: DEPARTURE DATE   PORT: RETURN DATE   PORT:

BATTLES, ENGAGEMENTS, SKIRMISHES, EXPEDITIONS: COMMANDING OFFICERS: CITATIONS:

WOUNDS RECEIVED IN SERVICE; SICKNESS OR HOSPITALIZATION:

IMPORTANT LEAVES OR FURLOUGHS:

DISCHARGED AT OR SEPARATION.

NAME _____ SERVICE NUMBER: _____ JOB CLASSIFICATION: _____

ENLISTED OR INDUCTED: _____ MONTH: _____ DAY: _____ YEAR: _____ AT AGE _____

BRANCH OF SERVICE _____ GRADE _____

TRAINING CAMPS _____ SERVICE SCHOOLS ATTENDED: _____

_____

_____

_____

DIVISION: _____ REGIMENT: _____ DEPARTMENT OR SHIP: _____ DATES _____

COMPANY: _____ TRANSFERRED: _____

_____

PROMOTIONS AND DATES: _____

_____

_____

_____

OVERSEAS SERVICE: _____ DEPARTURE DATE _____ PORT: _____ RETURN DATE _____ PORT: _____

_____

_____

_____

_____

BATTLES, ENGAGEMENTS, SKIRMISHES, EXPEDITIONS: _____ COMMANDING OFFICERS: _____ CITATIONS: _____

_____

_____

_____

WOUNDS RECEIVED IN SERVICE; SICKNESS OR HOSPITALIZATION: _____

_____

_____

IMPORTANT LEAVES OR FURLOUGHS: _____

_____

DISCHARGED AT OR SEPARATION. _____

Military Service Records CONTINUED

NAME

SERVICE NUMBER :

JOB CLASSIFICATION :

ENLISTED OR INDUCTED:

MONTH: DAY: YEAR: AT   AGE

BRANCH OF SERVICE   GRADE

TRAINING CAMPS   SERVICE SCHOOLS ATTENDED:

DIVISION: REGIMENT: DEPARTMENT OR SHIP: DATES

COMPANY: TRANSFERRED:

PROMOTIONS AND DATES:

OVERSEAS SERVICE: DEPARTURE DATE   PORT: RETURN DATE   PORT:

BATTLES, ENGAGEMENTS, SKIRMISHES, EXPEDITIONS: COMMANDING OFFICERS: CITATIONS:

WOUNDS RECEIVED IN SERVICE; SICKNESS OR HOSPITALIZATION:

IMPORTANT LEAVES OR FURLOUGHS:

DISCHARGED AT OR SEPARATION.

NAME _____ SERVICE NUMBER: _____ JOB CLASSIFICATION: _____

ENLISTED OR INDUCTED: _____ MONTH: _____ DAY: _____ YEAR: _____ AT AGE _____

BRANCH OF SERVICE _____ GRADE _____

TRAINING CAMPS _____ SERVICE SCHOOLS ATTENDED: _____

_____

_____

_____

DIVISION: _____ REGIMENT: _____ DEPARTMENT OR SHIP: _____ DATES _____

COMPANY: _____ TRANSFERRED: _____

_____

PROMOTIONS AND DATES: _____

_____

_____

_____

_____

OVERSEAS SERVICE: _____ DEPARTURE DATE _____ PORT: _____ RETURN DATE _____ PORT: _____

_____

_____

_____

_____

BATTLES, ENGAGEMENTS, SKIRMISHES, EXPEDITIONS: _____ COMMANDING OFFICERS: _____ CITATIONS: _____

_____

_____

_____

_____

WOUNDS RECEIVED IN SERVICE; SICKNESS OR HOSPITALIZATION: _____

_____

_____

IMPORTANT LEAVES OR FURLOUGHS: _____

_____

DISCHARGED AT OR SEPARATION. _____

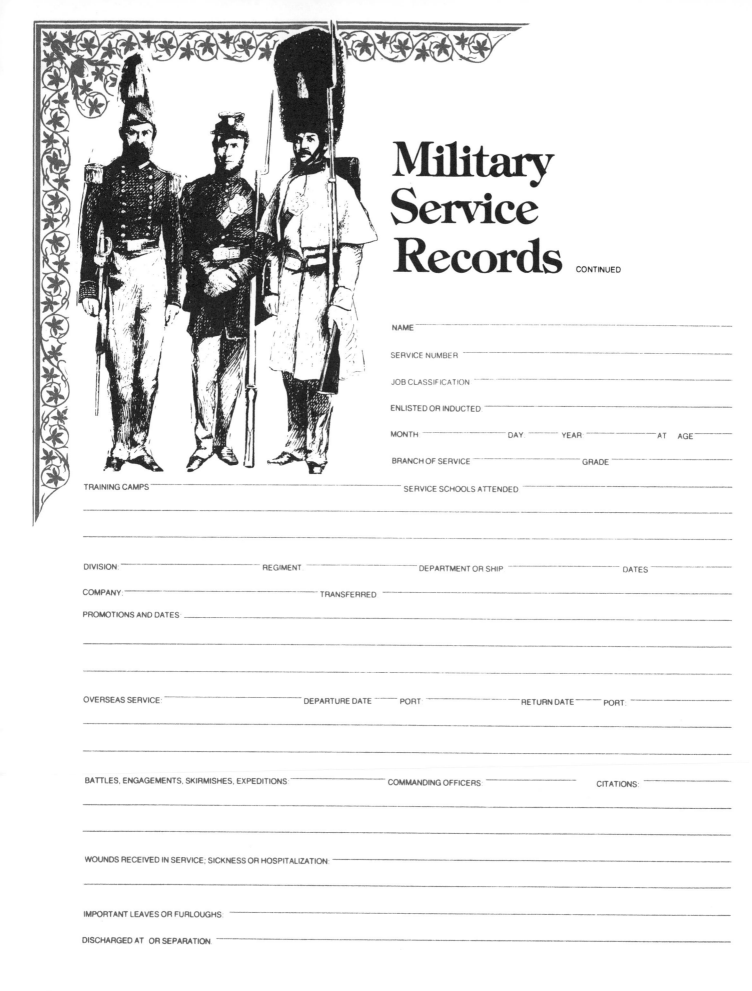

Military Service Records CONTINUED

NAME _____

SERVICE NUMBER _____

JOB CLASSIFICATION _____

ENLISTED OR INDUCTED: _____

MONTH _____ DAY _____ YEAR _____ AT AGE _____

BRANCH OF SERVICE _____ GRADE _____

TRAINING CAMPS _____ SERVICE SCHOOLS ATTENDED _____

_____

_____

DIVISION: _____ REGIMENT _____ DEPARTMENT OR SHIP _____ DATES _____

COMPANY: _____ TRANSFERRED _____

PROMOTIONS AND DATES: _____

_____

_____

OVERSEAS SERVICE: _____ DEPARTURE DATE ____ PORT _____ RETURN DATE ____ PORT: _____

_____

_____

BATTLES, ENGAGEMENTS, SKIRMISHES, EXPEDITIONS: _____ COMMANDING OFFICERS: _____ CITATIONS: _____

_____

_____

WOUNDS RECEIVED IN SERVICE; SICKNESS OR HOSPITALIZATION: _____

_____

IMPORTANT LEAVES OR FURLOUGHS: _____

DISCHARGED AT OR SEPARATION: _____

NAME _____ SERVICE NUMBER: _____ JOB CLASSIFICATION: _____

ENLISTED OR INDUCTED: _____ MONTH: _____ DAY: _____ YEAR: _____ AT   AGE _____

BRANCH OF SERVICE _____ GRADE _____

TRAINING CAMPS _____ SERVICE SCHOOLS ATTENDED: _____

_____

_____

_____

DIVISION: _____ REGIMENT: _____ DEPARTMENT OR SHIP: _____ DATES _____

COMPANY: _____ TRANSFERRED: _____

_____

PROMOTIONS AND DATES: _____

_____

_____

_____

OVERSEAS SERVICE: _____ DEPARTURE DATE _____ PORT: _____ RETURN DATE _____ PORT: _____

_____

_____

_____

_____

BATTLES, ENGAGEMENTS, SKIRMISHES, EXPEDITIONS: _____ COMMANDING OFFICERS: _____ CITATIONS: _____

_____

_____

_____

WOUNDS RECEIVED IN SERVICE; SICKNESS OR HOSPITALIZATION: _____

_____

_____

IMPORTANT LEAVES OR FURLOUGHS: _____

_____

DISCHARGED AT OR SEPARATION. _____

Special Friends

Everyone has a best friend who sometimes seems a part of the family. Certainly they make up some big parts of your life, so including them in a family record book seems appropriate. Don't forget to include dates, addresses and some of those things that make these people so special.

Our Pets

The chances are millions to one that you have a pet elephant but more than likely you have a dog, cat, turtle or fish. Animals, like good friends, seem to become part of the family and play a part in our daily lives. Because they are integrated into the 'family,' remembering them will recall fond memories.

OWNER	PET'S NAME	TYPE OF PET	DATES OF OWNERSHIP

Family Automobiles

OWNER	MAKE, MODEL, YEAR	COLOR	DATES OF OWNERSHIP
_____	_____	_____	_____
_____	_____	_____	_____
_____	_____	_____	_____
_____	_____	_____	_____
_____	_____	_____	_____
_____	_____	_____	_____
_____	_____	_____	_____
_____	_____	_____	_____
_____	_____	_____	_____
_____	_____	_____	_____

Americans have always been a people on the move and ever since Henry Ford started to mass produce cars they have been a part of almost every family's life. Every auto you have owned or will own has a special place in your life and remembering them will bring back lots of memories.

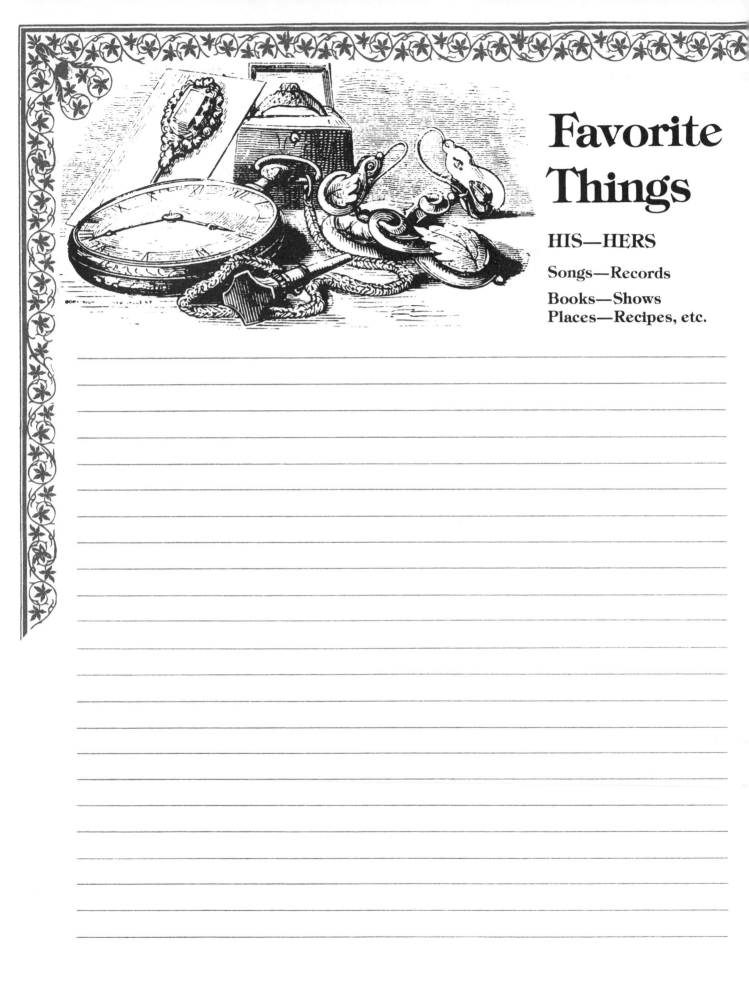

Favorite Things

HIS—HERS

Songs—Records

Books—Shows
Places—Recipes, etc.

CHILDREN

Songs—Records
Stories—Toys
Places—Pastimes, etc.

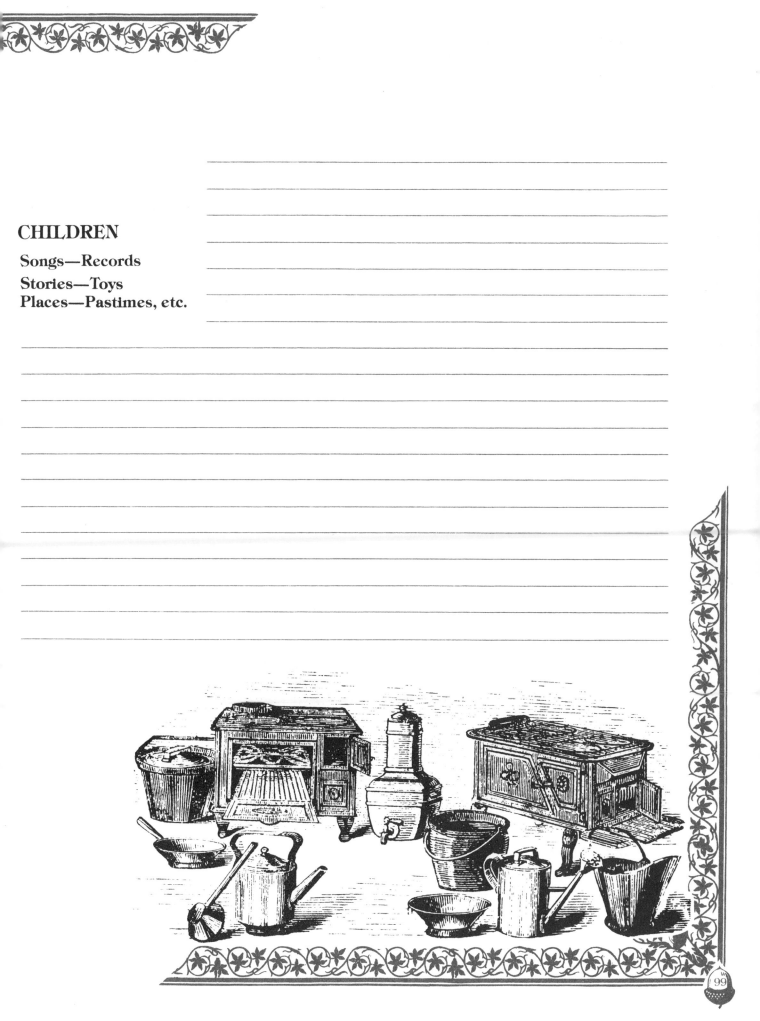

Collections and Heirlooms

Include here special collections of various family members—what they are, when begun, how much collected, etc. List all heirlooms, including original owner and how items were passed from generation to generation. In short, record anything of interest to you that will also be of interest to others who read about your family.

Collections and Heirlooms

CONTINUED

Favorite Family Sports

FAMILY OR INDIVIDUAL'S NAME	SPORT, TEAM, CLUB	SPECIAL ACHIEVEMENT

Favorite Family Sports CONTINUED

From woodcarving and quilt making to rebuilding old cars and raising exotic plants, many families have individuals who pursue a wide variety of interesting hobbies. Here is space to record those individuals and their pastimes and any fascinating pieces of information about how they started and why and whether anyone else followed in their footsteps.

Favorite Family Hobbies

Favorite Family Hobbies

_____

_____

_____

_____

_____

_____

_____

_____

_____

_____

_____

_____

_____

_____

_____

_____

_____

_____

_____

_____

_____

_____

_____

_____

_____

_____

_____

Family Vacations

Getting away from it all seems to keep us
going through the rest of the year so entering
some of the places you go to, who was there,
and what happened can help bring back some
of that fun. Some vacations are not so much
where you went as what you did or who you
met , so by recording this you have the chance,
in the future, to look back and smile or cry.

Family
Reunions

Remembering who was there and at what occasion is a lot easier if you record it here. In years to come this kind of information will conjure up the event all over again for you. No matter whether it was your fifth high school class reunion or the family's Fiftieth Wedding Anniversary.

who was there

Family Reunions CONTINUED

Family Traditions

Events
to Remember

Here you may record information about events (other than such things as reunions, trips, and club activities) that you may want to recall years from now. Include family "firsts" and unique achievements—winning a special prize, meeting a famed personality, or witnessing an outstanding event.

Events to Remember CONTINUED

Oral Family History

From survivors and participants in wars to migrations from other countries, each family has stories no one has ever written down. Here is space to do so to record forever what will be lost if it remains "oral history."

_____
_____
_____
_____
_____
_____
_____
_____
_____
_____
_____
_____
_____
_____
_____
_____
_____
_____
_____
_____

Oral
Family
History

CONTINUED

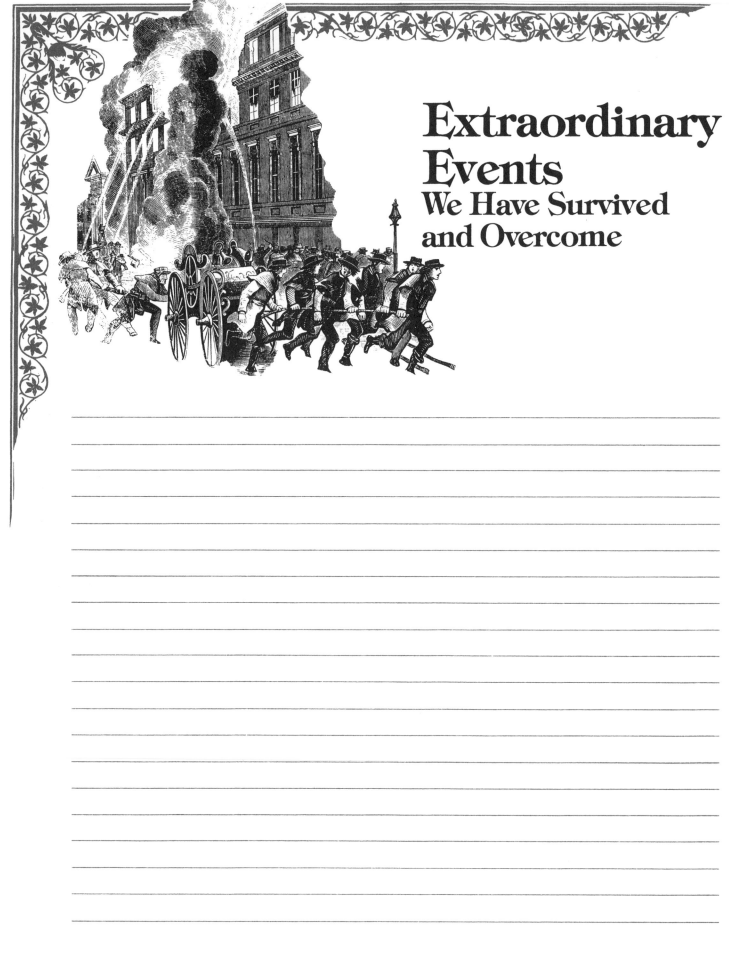

Extraordinary
Events
We Have Survived
and Overcome

Into each family come those unforeseen events.
Many have survived natural disasters (floods,
tornados) and many times families were forced
to move or lives were altered for the better as a
result. Here is space for you to record whatever
you feel is appropriate in relation to your own
family's experiences.

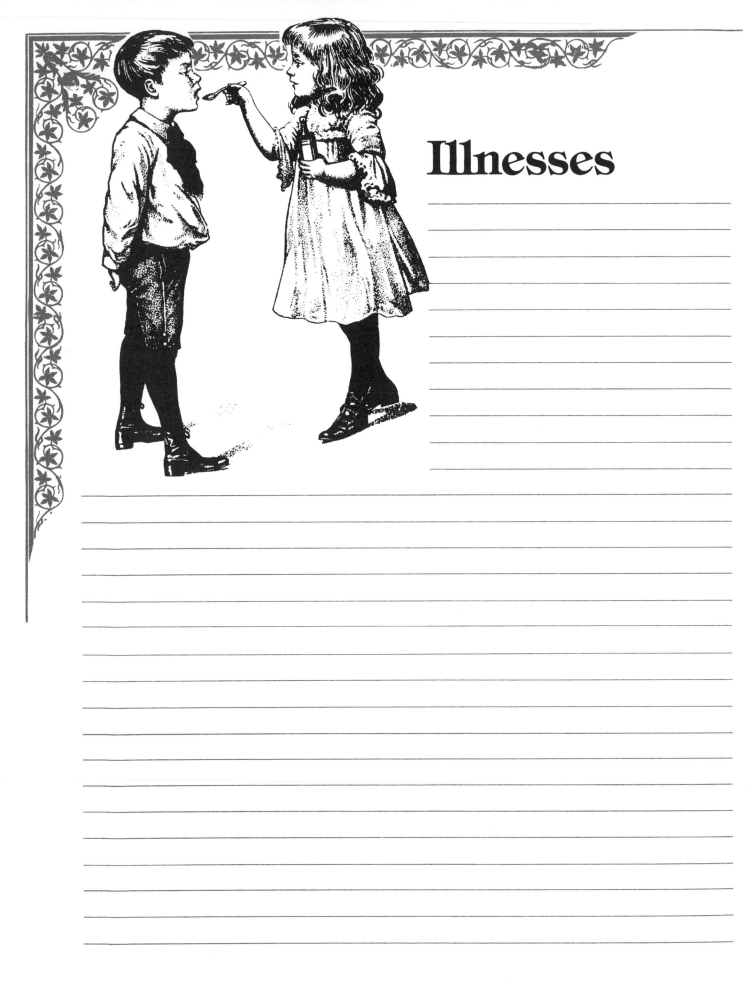

Illnesses

NAME	ILLNESS, OPERATION	HOSPITAL, DOCTOR	DATE

HIS _____

 Height _____

 Weight _____

 Hair Color _____

 Color of Eyes _____

 Suit Size _____

 Shirt Size _____

 Waist _____

 Shoe Size _____

 Hat Size _____

 Ring Size _____

 Other Sizes _____

_____

_____

_____

_____

_____

_____

_____

Color Preference _____

_____

_____

_____

_____

Toiletries Preference _____

_____

Vital Statistics

Space is provided on these pages for vital statistics. Fill in with as much detail as you care to note.

_____
_____
_____
_____

Other Sizes _____

HERS _____

Height _____

Weight _____

Hair Color _____

Color of Eyes _____

Blouse Size _____

Dress Size _____

Shoe Size _____

Ring Size _____

_____
_____
_____
_____
_____
_____
_____

Color Preference _____

_____
_____
_____

Perfume & Toiletries Preference _____

_____
_____

Vital Statistics CONTINUED

CHILDREN	Height	Weight	Hair Color	Color of Eye

Color Preference

Suit Size Dress Size	Blouse Size Shirt Size	Shoe Size	Hat Size	Ring Size	Other Sizes

Photographs

Pictures do their own story telling and in years to come a lot can be learned from this kind of record. You and future generations will be able to look back and see a member of the family in his or her own time and place. (You may also want to include favorite clippings, mementos, or documents.)

Photographs

CONTINUED

Photographs

CONTINUED

GENEALOGY RESEARCH

All of us know something about our living relatives. We enjoy telling stories about their achievements and exploits, and we certainly have a fondness for the endearing characters that are in most families. Yet our knowledge of our families often does not go beyond those members we actually know. Few of us have been lucky enough to have known our great-grandparents for example. This shows us that one of the most common ways of learning about ourselves is by word of mouth; the so-called oral tradition. Thus, if you want to begin finding out more about your family the place to start is with your relatives. Ask them if they can provide you with birth dates, places of residence and dates of death of those whom you do not know, such as your great-grandparents. Do this as far as it is possible to trace them. Also, check to see if there are any relatives who have previously done genealogical research that might aid in your search. Once you have reached this point you will discover the great treasures of information available in family bibles, picture, albums, old letters, diaries and account books. Your ancestors often kept better records than you think!

OUR FAMILY TREE

If you have access to a computer, search the Internet for surnames you have found (mother's maiden name, grandmother's maiden name, etc.) You might discover some useful information or even come across others who are doing research on the same lines of genealogy as you. There are many websites and message boards devoted entirely to genealogy. Check them out, look for surnames, get what help you can from them.

Once you have names, dates and places you can consult town records. Securing birth certificates, marriage licenses, death certificates, wills and land deeds will give you additional names you will want and need. Don't be disappointed if some of these public records are not available. You can always check your public library. Some of the subjects you can look up at the library are clans, deeds, epitaphs, estates, marriage licenses, nobility, parish registers, peerage and precedence. Also don't forget to ask the librarian for additional sources of genealogical information. If the books listed in the card catalogue are not in the stacks, your librarian can easily send for them.

Another place to check is your state genealogical association or historical society. Each state has its own organization with qualified people who can be very helpful in local matters. These associations also often publish their own periodicals that you might like to look into. The Daughters of the American Revolution in your area may also be able to furnish you with further information. Sometimes they too publish interesting pamphlets on the subject.

The next step in your search is to contact the National Archives, which is the central United States depository for records, located in Washington, D.C., to find out which of their eleven regional branches is nearest you. The National Archives contain many different kinds of records which will be helpful to you. The Census Records, from 1790 to date, are kept here. They give information such as the name of each family member, age, occupation and place of birth. Also available are records of military service, pensions and land grants. Since we are a nation of immigrants you may find here the names of the first members of your family who came to America, as well as the name of the ship that brought them, the date of arrival, the port of entry and the date of naturalization. For other such information one should consult the United States Immigration and Naturalization office.

For the majority of us our families have only lived in America for three or four generations. It was about this time that the mass immigrations from other countries to the United States began. Thus far, all of the research information has concentrated on relatives who lived in America. There is no need to stop researching at this point however, because there are sources available to help you trace your ancestors to the countries that they originally came from. The library of the Church of Jesus Christ of Latter-Day Saints in Salt Lake City contains the largest collection of genealogical information dating from 1538 to 1805. It contains records from the national and local archives, courthouses, cemeteries, churches and a variety of other places where records were kept, about people all over the world. Some 40 countries are represented in this collection of genealogical data. This enormous library has branches around the world and since they require that you do your own research you can contact them to find out which of the twenty branches is closest to you. The library's researchers are continually making copies of genealogical records throughout the world to further expand the collection.

For the most part, at this point your have completed all of the research that can be done in America and it is time to write away to foreign countries to get additional information. To find out where and to whom to write you should contact the consulate of the country to which you are writing. Once the consulate has sent you the correct address and the name of the person to whom you should write, do not hesitate because you don't speak the language; the agency will get someone to translate your letter for them. It is very important to include as much perti-

nent information as you have. Names, dates, places of residence are especially necessary. One thing you must consider is that often when people arrived in America from other countries their names were misspelled or arbitrarily anglicized and therefore you must know what their name was originally before you make any inquiries.

Do not get discouraged, as you can see there are many sources to help you find information. To give you an idea of what results your search for your roots can lead to, let us take an historical example. It has been over 350 years since the arrival of the Mayflower in 1620, which means there have been about 13 generations of your family since that time. These 13 generations represent more than 16,000 direct descendants.

To account for all of these ancestors in order to have a complete genealogical chart would be an imposing task even for an expert and, if you continued to expand the charts used in this book, by the time you reached 1600 that column would have over 8,000 spaces for names and be over 165 feet tall. If you decide after doing some searching on your own that you need the help of a professional researcher, research and contact qualified genealogists. Some people who did not have a written language will have to rely on the records of others. To say the least, at most times they are inaccurate and distorted. Even the South American Indians, who did have a written language, lost it, so all natives of the Western Hemisphere and Black Africans will have to seek out oral family or tribal histories which many times cannot pinpoint a place, person, or date but in general are quite close to fact. Do not be taken in by the commercially advertised mail-order coat-of-arms trade.

The charts that appear in this book go back five generations, about 150 years. These five generations represent about 124 people in a direct line descendancy.

Where to write for booklets on how and where to find vital records:

Superintendent of Documents
United States Government Printing Office
732 N. Capital St., NW
Washington, D.C. 20402
Ph: 1-888-293-6498
http://bookstore.gpo.gov
"Where to Write for Vital Records:
Births, Deaths, and Divorces" 2003
(Public Health Service Publication, $4.25)

The Church of Jesus Christ of Latter-Day Saints
50 E. North Temple Street
Salt Lake City, Utah 84150
Ph: 1-801-240-1000
www.familysearch.org

The National Archives and Records Administration
8601 Adelphi Road

College Park, MD 20740-6001
Ph: 1-866-272-6272
www.archives.gov

Board for the Certification of Genealogists
P.O Box 14291
Washington, D.C. 20044
www.bcgcertification.org

BOOKSTORES WHICH SPECIALIZE IN GENEALOGICAL MATERIAL

Genealogical Publishing Co., Inc.
1001 N. Calvert Street
Baltimore, MD 21202-3897
Ph: 1-800-296-6687
Fax: 1-410-752-8492
Orders: sales@genealogical.com
www.genealogical.com

Higginson Book Company
148 Washington Street
Salem, MA 01970
Ph: 1-978-745-7170
Fax: 1-978-745-8025
Orders: orders@higginsonbooks.com
www.higginsonbooks.com

Tuttle Antiquarian Books Inc.
28 South Main Street
Rutland, VT 05701
Ph: 1-802-773-8229
Fax: 1-802-773-1493
Contact: tuttbook@sover.net
www.tuttlebooks.com

Willow Bend Books Bookstore
Customer Service Division
65 E. Main Street
Westminster, MD 21157
Ph: 1-800-876-6103
Fax: 1-410-871-2674
Contact: info@heritagebooks.com
www.heritagebooks.com

PUBLICATIONS:

Family Chronicle Magazine
(www.familychronicle.com)

Family Tree Magazine
(www.familytreemagazine.com)

Everton's Family History Magazine
(www.everton.com)

Eastman's Online Genealogy Newsletter
(www.eogn.com)

Heritage Quest
(www.heritagequest.com)

Journal of Online Genealogy
(www.onlinegenealogy.com)

Ancestor News
(www.ancestornews.com)

HELPFUL WEBSITES

www.cyndislist.com (Guide, information, websites, tips)
www.ancestry.com (Genealogy)
www.rootsweb.com (Genealogy)
www.onegreatfamily.com (Genealogy)
www.genealogytoday.com (Genealogy)
www.genealogytoday.com/ca (Genealogy, Canadian)
www.ellisisland.org (Ellis Island)
www.usgenweb.org (USGenWeb Project)

www.rootsweb.com/~canwgw/ (Canada GenWeb Project)
www.loc.gov/rr/genealogy (Library of Congress)
www.ingeneas.com (Genealogy, Canadian)
www.acgs.org (American-Canadian Genealogical Society)
www.collectionscanada.ca (Library and Archives Canada)
www.allvitalrecords.com (Birth, census, marriage, death records)
http://newspaperarchive.com (Searchable newspapers dating back to 1748)

BIBLIOGRAPHY

American Genealogical Research Institute. **How to Trace Your Family Tree**. Dolphin Books.

Bennett, Archibald F. **Finding Your Forefathers in America**. Salt Lake City, Bookcraft Co., 1957.

Bidlack, Russell Eugene. **First Steps in Climbing the Family Tree**. Detroit Society for Genealogical Research, 1966.

Doane, Gilbert H. **Searching for Your Ancestors**. New York, Bantam Books, Inc., 1974.

Everton, George B. **The Handybook for Genealogist**. Logan, Utah, Everton Publishers, 1962.

Greenwood, Val D. **The Researcher's Guide to American Genealogy**. Genealogical Publishing Co., 1973.

Iredale, David. **Discovering Your Family Tree**. Shire Publications.

National Genealogical Society. Special Publications: No. 17, **Genealogy, Handmaid of History**.
(A list can be obtained of other articles on the subject from the Society, 1921 Sunderland Place, N.W., Washington, D.C. 20036)

Rottenberg, Dan. **Finding Our Fathers**. New York, Random House, 1977.

Williams, Ethel W. **Know Your Ancestors**. Rutland, Vt., C.E. Tuttle Co., 1964.